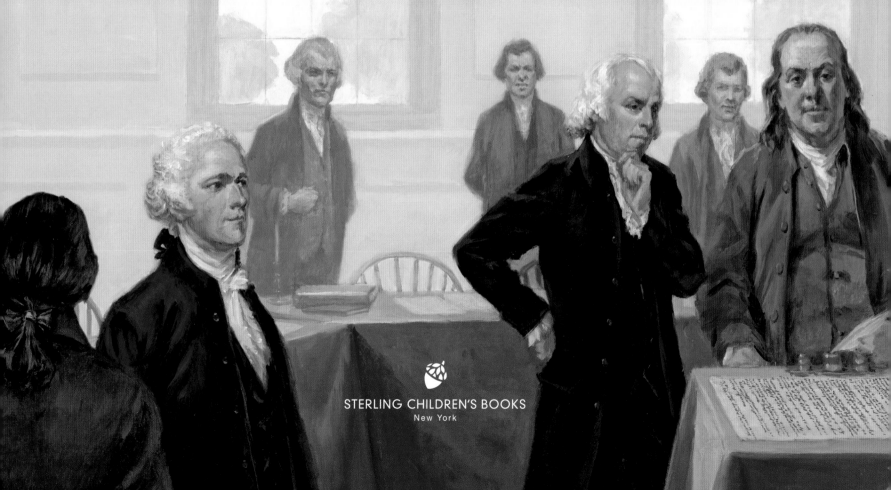

Good Question!

What Are the Three
Branches of Government?
AND OTHER QUESTIONS ABOUT . . .
the U.S. Constitution

STERLING CHILDREN'S BOOKS
New York

STERLING CHILDREN'S BOOKS
New York

An Imprint of Sterling Publishing
387 Park Avenue South
New York, NY 10016

Image Credits
10 top left and bottom: Harvard Law School Library; 10 top right: Yale University Art Gallery/Courtesy Yale University; 11 top left and center: National Gallery of Art; 11 top right: Washington University Law School/Courtesy Wikimedia Foundation; 11 bottom left: White House Historical Association/Courtesy Wikimedia Foundation; 11 bottom center: National Archives; 11 bottom right: © traveler1116/iStockphoto; 15: Architect of the Capitol; 16: National Archives; 19: © Tim Sloan/AFP/Getty Images; 20: © miralex/iStockphoto; 23: © Chip Somodevilla/Getty Images

ISBN 978-1-4549-1243-9 [hardcover]
ISBN 978-1-4549-1244-6 [paperback]

Distributed in Canada by Sterling Publishing
c/o Canadian Manda Group, 165 Dufferin Street
Toronto, Ontario, Canada M6K 3H6
Distributed in the United Kingdom by GMC Distribution Services
Castle Place, 166 High Street, Lewes, East Sussex, England BN7 1XU
Distributed in Australia by Capricorn Link (Australia) Pty. Ltd.
P.O. Box 704, Windsor, NSW 2756, Australia

Design by Andrea Miller
Paintings by Wilson Ong

For information about custom editions, special sales, and premium and corporate purchases, please contact Sterling Special Sales at 800-805-5489 or specialsales@sterlingpublishing.com.

Manufactured in China
Lot #:
2 4 6 8 10 9 7 5 3 1
10/14

www.sterlingpublishing.com/kids

CONTENTS

What is a constitution? 4

Did the United States exist before the Constitution? 7

Did a group of angry farmers almost topple America? 8

What was wrong with the Articles of the Confederation? 8

Who attended the Constitutional Convention? 10

Who was the Father of the Constitution? 13

How long did it take to write the Constitution? 14

What is in the Constitution? 17

What is the preamble? 17

What are the three branches of government? 18

Who leads the executive branch? 21

Who is appointed to be a judge for life? 22

How long did it take to approve the Constitution? 24

Who was the first president? 24

Has the Constitution changed? 26

What is the Bill of Rights? 27

Can amendments be taken back? 28

What are other famous amendments? 29

What is the future for the Constitution? 30

Constitution Timeline 32

What is a constitution?

In the National Archives Museum in Washington, D.C., you can see the original United States Constitution. The room is dim and a security guard stands on duty as more than one million people each year visit this special document in its glass display case. Why pay so much attention to a yellowed, old piece of parchment? What is a constitution anyway?

A constitution is the set of rules for a country. It outlines how a government works, what it does for its people, and what its people do for the government. Many constitutions say how the people's leaders will be selected and what power those leaders have.

Before constitutions, many countries had codes of law. Some were written by only one person, and others weren't written down at all. That meant that sometimes the laws weren't fair to the people. In England, in 1215, a group of rich landowners and church leaders made King John sign a code of laws called the Magna Carta. It limited the king's powers and protected his subjects. For example, the king could no longer throw someone in jail without a trial. The Magna Carta became an important influence on the United States Constitution.

In this book, the "constitution" refers to the United States Constitution, even though there are many constitutions in the world. New constitutions are still being written. In 2014, Tunisia signed a new constitution. The oldest constitution was signed into law by the tiny country of San Marino in 1600, but most historians agree that the United States Constitution is the oldest single-document constitution still used today.

The longest written constitution in the world belongs to the country of India. It has thirty-two parts, three hundred ninety-five articles, and ninety-eight amendments. It is kept in a container full of helium for protection. With just seven articles and twenty-seven amendments, the United States Constitution is the shortest written constitution. Signed—or ratified—into law in 1788, the US Constitution became a model for many constitutions that came after it.

In 1215, King John met with English barons and church leaders at Runnymead to sign the Charter of Liberties—also known as the Magna Carta.

Did the United States exist before the Constitution?

According to legend, when the Revolutionary War was beginning, Benjamin Franklin told the thirteen colonies, "We must hang together, or assuredly we shall all hang separately." He was telling the colonies that they needed to work together to be rid of British rule; otherwise, they would lose the war for their freedom. So, in the middle of the revolution, leaders from each of the colonies met in York, Pennsylvania. They wrote the Articles of the Confederation, the United States' first code of laws. The colonial leaders called themselves the Congress of the Confederation, and agreed to meet after the war to make new laws for the colonies. In the articles, the colonies vowed to protect each other and treat each other's citizens well. They decided that Congress would make deals with foreign countries and that the Articles of Confederation could not be changed unless all the colonies agreed.

After winning the Revolutionary War against the British, the United States of America was sovereign—no other country ruled over it. But the young country wasn't as unified then as it is today. Each of the thirteen colonies had its own constitution, its own rulers, and even its own money. Can you imagine living in Massachusetts and not being able to use your money to buy something in Rhode Island? Meanwhile, the federal government, which looked over the whole country rather than a single state, was very small. What's more, there wasn't much of an army for the country, only for the states. The federal government did not have the power to collect taxes, so it couldn't pay an army, and relied on states for money. The states didn't always pay on time, and so the federal government could not always do its job. Something needed to change.

Did a group of angry farmers almost topple America?

After the revolution, the United States was in rough shape. Prices for everything were higher, and farmers in particular were struggling with money. During this time, owing too much money could get you sent to jail! Many farmers like Daniel Shays had just returned from fighting the British and felt like they deserved better treatment. Shays came home from the war to find that he had to go to court for unpaid debt. He began organizing protests for "debt relief," so he and others would not have to go to jail. But the Massachusetts state government went on break without considering debt relief. Shays and other protestors surrounded the county courthouse in protest.

Merchants in Massachusetts didn't want debt relief, because the farmers owed them money. So, when the Massachusetts government couldn't fund an army to defend the courthouse, merchants hired three thousand men to work like an army. These men fired cannons at the farmers, killing four, wounding twenty, and scattering the rest. The Massachusetts government eventually forgave the people who participated in the rebellion, including Daniel Shays.

Shays' Rebellion scared people around the country. It showed that state governments weren't ready to deal with a rebellion on their own, but they also could not rely on other states for help.

What was wrong with the Articles of the Confederation?

The Articles of the Confederation that were written during the Revolutionary War made the federal government weak. It could not collect taxes or fund its own army. There was no strong Navy to protect United States ships from pirates, and no president to make trade agreements with other countries. Even sending goods between states was difficult. So, in 1786, former Congressman Alexander Hamilton led a meeting of representatives from five different states in Annapolis, Maryland. They agreed that the United States needed a stronger federal government. They decided to meet in Philadelphia, Pennsylvania, with members from every state, to create a constitution.

Who attended the Constitutional Convention?

Fifty-five delegates attended the Convention. Some wanted a country with strong state governments.

William Paterson— New Jersey
Paterson proposed the New Jersey Plan, which said that all states should get the same number of votes in the new federal government.

Roger Sherman— Connecticut
Sherman was behind the Great Compromise, which led to Congress having two houses.

Luther Martin— Maryland
Martin was worried that the big states would push around the little states. He also walked out of the convention after no one supported his idea for a bill of rights.

Gunning Bedford— Delaware
Bedford warned that if the small states weren't represented in the United States government, they would find help from foreign governments.

FEDERALISTS

Other delegates wanted a more united country with a stronger federal government.

James Madison—Virginia
Madison is called the Father of the Constitution and was the first to arrive at the Constitutional Convention.

George Washington—Virginia
Washington, the famous Revolutionary War general who led the colonial army to victory, was elected leader of the convention.

Alexander Hamilton—New York
Hamilton, born in the West Indies, would go on to become the first secretary of the treasury.

Benjamin Franklin—Pennsylvania
Franklin was the oldest member of the Constitutional Convention, at eighty-one years old. Some people call him the First American because he worked so hard to unite the colonies.

Robert Morris—Pennsylvania
Although Morris was born in England, he signed the Declaration of Independence, the Articles of Confederation, and the Constitution.

Gouverneur Morris—Pennsylvania
It is thought that Morris wrote the preamble to the Constitution. He is also called the Penman of the Constitution because he wrote large sections of it.

Who was the Father of the Constitution?

The first delegate to arrive at the Constitutional Convention was James Madison. A short man from Virginia who loved to read, thirty-six-year-old Madison was excited to replace the Articles of Confederation. He had already helped to write Virginia's state constitution in 1776. George Washington arrived from Virginia soon after Madison. He was a famous general, and the people of Philadelphia cheered as they saw him coming.

The spring was very rainy and many of the roads had turned to mud, so few delegates were on time. While they waited for more delegates to arrive, Madison wrote the Virginia Plan with some input from his fellow Virginians. The plan called for a government that was voted in by the people and had three parts: a congress to make laws, a court to make decisions about laws, and a president to be the chief diplomat and head of the armed forces. The states would choose whom to send to Congress, but the number of people they were allowed to send would depend on how many people lived in the state.

By May of 1787 the delegates had all finally arrived. They voted for Washington to lead the convention. Madison agreed to write down everything that was said. He was present at every meeting, and only stopped writing when he himself had something to say. When the convention finally began, Edmund Randolph quickly introduced Madison's Virginia Plan. The delegates used it as the blueprint for the Constitution and got to work making changes and adjustments. When all was done, James Madison was called the Father of the Constitution.

How long did it take to write the Constitution?

It became clear early on that the biggest question was how states would be represented in the new federal government. The bigger states supported the Virginia Plan. They thought the larger the state, the more representatives it should have in Congress. The smaller states supported the New Jersey Plan. They wanted every state to send an equal number of congressmen to the new government, so every state would have an equal say.

The delegates fought about this for weeks and weeks. The summer was boiling hot, but to keep their work secret, the delegates kept all the windows of the convention hall closed. Behind the locked doors of the hall tempers flared, but the delegates did not quit. They knew they had to get the Constitution right.

Finally in July, the delegates who wanted the Virginia Plan and the delegates who wanted the New Jersey Plan each agreed to give something up to work together. The new plan was called the Great Compromise. It blended the two plans, and created two "houses" of the legislative branch of the government—one where all states were equal and one where the number of votes each state got depended on the population of the state.

But the Great Compromise didn't resolve a big disagreement between the states in the South and the states in the North. There were over 600,000 black men and women in the United States at the time, and most were enslaved in the South. The southern states felt that these enslaved people should count toward their states' population size. This would give states in the South more power in the new government. The states in the North felt that since enslaved people were not allowed to say where they lived, would not get to vote, and did not have other rights, that they should not be counted. Another compromise was made: an enslaved person would count for three-fifths of a person. This was called the Three-fifths Compromise.

The delegates debated from May through September 17, 1787, even after the writers finished the first draft of the Constitution on August 6th. Finally, a young man named Jacob Shallus was paid $30 to write the famous Constitution onto the parchment you can see in the National Archives today.

Howard Chandler Christy's famous painting of the founders signing the Constitution was created in 1940. It hangs in the US Capitol Building in Washington DC.

We the People

of the United States, in Order to form a more perfect Union, establish Justice, insure domestic Tranquility, provide for the common defence, promote the general Welfare, and secure the Blessings of Liberty to ourselves and our Posterity, do ordain and establish this Constitution for the United States of America.

Article. I.

Section. 1. All legislative Powers herein granted shall be vested in a Congress of the United States, which shall consist of a Senate and House of Representatives.

Section. 2. The House of Representatives shall be composed of Members chosen every second Year by the People of the several States, and the Electors in each State shall have the Qualifications requisite for Electors of the most numerous Branch of the State Legislature.

No Person shall be a Representative who shall not have attained to the Age of twenty five Years, and been seven Years a Citizen of the United States, and who shall not, when elected, be an Inhabitant of that State in which he shall be chosen.

Representatives and direct Taxes shall be apportioned among the several States which may be included within this Union, according to their respective Numbers, which shall be determined by adding to the whole Number of free Persons, including those bound to Service for a Term of Years, and excluding Indians not taxed, three fifths of all other Persons. The actual Enumeration shall be made within three Years after the first Meeting of the Congress of the United States, and within every subsequent Term of ten Years, in such Manner as they shall by Law direct. The Number of Representatives shall not exceed one for every thirty Thousand, but each State shall have at Least one Representative; and until such enumeration shall be made, the State of New Hampshire shall be entitled to chuse three, Massachusetts eight, Rhode-Island and Providence Plantations one, Connecticut five, New-York six, New Jersey four, Pennsylvania eight, Delaware one, Maryland six, Virginia ten, North Carolina five, South Carolina five, and Georgia three.

When vacancies happen in the Representation from any State, the Executive Authority thereof shall issue Writs of Election to fill such Vacancies.

The House of Representatives shall chuse their Speaker and other Officers; and shall have the sole Power of Impeachment.

Section. 3. The Senate of the United States shall be composed of two Senators from each State, chosen by the Legislature thereof, for six Years; and each Senator shall have one Vote.

Immediately after they shall be assembled in Consequence of the first Election, they shall be divided as equally as may be into three Classes. The Seats of the Senators of the first Class shall be vacated at the Expiration of the second Year, of the second Class at the Expiration of the fourth Year, and of the third Class at the Expiration of the sixth Year, so that one third may be chosen every second Year; and if Vacancies happen by Resignation, or otherwise, during the Recess of the Legislature of any State, the Executive thereof may make temporary Appointments until the next Meeting of the Legislature, which shall then fill such Vacancies.

No Person shall be a Senator who shall not have attained to the Age of thirty Years, and been nine Years a Citizen of the United States, and who shall not, when elected, be an Inhabitant of that State for which he shall be chosen.

The Vice President of the United States shall be President of the Senate, but shall have no Vote, unless they be equally divided.

The Senate shall chuse their other Officers, and also a President pro tempore, in the Absence of the Vice President, or when he shall exercise the Office of President of the United States.

The Senate shall have the sole Power to try all Impeachments. When sitting for that Purpose, they shall be on Oath or Affirmation. When the President of the United States is tried, the Chief Justice shall preside: And no Person shall be convicted without the Concurrence of two thirds of the Members present.

Judgment in Cases of Impeachment shall not extend further than to removal from Office, and disqualification to hold and enjoy any Office of honor, Trust or Profit under the United States: but the Party convicted shall nevertheless be liable and subject to Indictment, Trial, Judgment and Punishment, according to Law.

Section. 4. The Times, Places and Manner of holding Elections for Senators and Representatives, shall be prescribed in each State by the Legislature thereof; but the Congress may at any time by Law make or alter such Regulations, except as to the Places of chusing Senators.

What is in the Constitution?

When the convention and all of the debating was over, Benjamin Franklin said, "I doubt too whether any other convention we can obtain, may be able to make a better Constitution."

The end result was a constitution with seven articles, or parts. The first three articles outline the separation of powers. The new Americans had just come from living under a king, and they wanted to make sure that no one person or group had too much control over the country. That's why the Constitution outlines what the federal government can and cannot do. Just like the Magna Carta, the Constitution says that you get a trial if you are accused of a crime. It also tells what the states can and cannot do—states can't declare war, for instance.

The Constitution also includes the rules for how it can be changed. Even after all of their hard work, the delegates knew the Constitution wasn't perfect. They wanted to make sure that it could always be improved. Still, Franklin was amazed at how well the final document came out. "It therefore astonishes me, Sir, to find this system approaching so near to perfection as it does; and I think it will astonish our enemies," he said.

What is the preamble?

The preamble is what begins the Constitution, and it is one of its most famous parts. It begins "We the people," and then explains that the document was written to form a country where people will be treated fairly, stay safe, and live together freely. Patrick Henry, who declined to attend the Constitutional Convention, was upset by the very first three words of the preamble. He thought Americans should be loyal to their states first. To him, Americans were not a "people" who could speak in one voice. But the Constitution explains how people can be citizens of both a state and a country at the same time.

What are the three branches of government?

The Constitution breaks the government up into three parts, or branches. They are called the legislative, executive, and judicial branches. The whole goal of this complicated system is to make sure that no one person or part of the government has too much power. This is called a system of "checks and balances."

The legislative branch is in charge of making laws. It is also called Congress. The Great Compromise was supposed to make both the big and the small states happy. Congress would have two different houses, or groups, of lawmakers. The two houses of Congress are the House of Representatives and the Senate.

The House of Representatives is made up of different numbers of representatives from every state. The more people living in the state, the more members it has in the House of Representatives. For example, Nebraska, a state with few people, sends three members to the House of Representatives. A much more populated state, Texas, sends thirty-six! The other house of Congress is called the Senate. Every state, from the smallest to the biggest, sends two senators to the Senate.

The job of Congress is to pass bills, which either make new laws or tell the government how to spend its money, which is called a budget. Every bill that the House of Representatives passes needs to also pass the Senate. Once it passes both houses, the bill goes on to the next branch of government.

This is the House of Representatives inside the US Capitol Building. The 441 representatives meet here to make laws.

The President of the United States lives in the White House in Washington DC.

Who leads the executive branch?

Once a bill passes through Congress, it goes to the president. The president is the executive branch of the government. The president cannot make laws, but it is his or her job to defend the Constitution. If the president doesn't think a law is right, he or she can refuse to sign it. This is called a "veto."

Article II of the Constitution explains what the executive branch of the government is. The president is elected every four years, but the people do not directly vote for who becomes president. Instead, the states choose electors based on how many senators and representatives it has. California has the most electors, 55, because it has the most people. Wyoming has the fewest people and has only three electoral votes. These electors vote for the president. You might be thinking, "but I've seen regular people vote for the president!" These people are voting to tell their state electors who to vote for. But this is not outlined in the Constitution.

While only Congress has the power to declare war, the president is in charge of the armed forces. This is why you might hear the president called "the commander in chief." These days most presidents leave military planning to their generals and advisors, but the president is still in charge. The president is also the country's chief diplomat, so he or she greets foreign leaders and discusses politics with them. President Jimmy Carter famously invited the presidents of Israel and Egypt to the United States in 1978, to help the two countries stop fighting.

The oath that the president says as he or she is sworn in can also be found in the Constitution. It goes, "I do solemnly swear (or affirm) that I will faithfully execute the Office of President of the United States, and will to the best of my ability, preserve, protect and defend the Constitution of the United States."

Who is appointed to be a judge for life?

nce a bill passes through Congress and is signed by the president, it becomes a law! But it can still be challenged or changed. If the law isn't clear, or if it violates the Constitution, the Supreme Court can step in. The Supreme Court represents the third branch of the government: the judicial branch.

The Supreme Court is the highest court in the US. It is sometimes called the "court of last resort" because people can appeal any other court's ruling and get another trial, but not after a Supreme Court ruling. If a case is so complicated or unusual that no other court can settle it, or if no law exists already, or if it looks like the law isn't clear, the case will sometimes go to the Supreme Court. Some people say that a president's longest lasting impact is whom he or she chooses for the Supreme Court. That's because once someone becomes a Supreme Court judge, also called a justice, they can stay for as long as they can do the job. William Orville Douglas served on the court for 36 years—there were nine presidential elections in that time! There are no elections for Supreme Court justices, so the process for choosing a new justice after an old one dies or retires can take a long time. It is the president's job to choose new justices.

There are nine Supreme Court justices so that there are no ties when they decide on a case. This isn't in the Constitution, so the number of justices has changed over time.

The third article of the Constitution says that the US Supreme Court decides if new laws or treaties are constitutional. If it is declared unconstitutional, a law must be replaced by a new law.

William Howard Taft is the only president to serve on the Supreme Court. After being president from 1909 to 1913, he became the chief justice in 1921. The first woman to be appointed to the Supreme Court was Sandra Day O'Connor. President Ronald Reagan appointed her in 1981.

Nine justices make up
the Supreme Court.

How long did it take to approve the Constitution?

lthough there were fifty-five delegates in total at the Constitutional Convention, only thirty-nine signed the Constitution. Some delegates would have signed the Constitution, but they were pulled home before it was ready. Some delegates left in anger because they didn't like what the Constitution was becoming. Three delegates who were present refused to sign the Constitution. Edmund Randolph, from Virginia, didn't sign because he thought the Constitution didn't have enough checks and balances. Elbridge Gerry, from Massachusetts, didn't think that the convention had the authority to reshape the country's government. And George Mason would not sign because the Constitution didn't include a bill of rights to protect the people.

After the Constitution was completed, copies were sent to all thirteen state governments. If nine of the thirteen states, or a two-thirds majority, voted for the new Constitution the new federal government would be approved. Every state set up its own constitutional convention to review the new Constitution. In December 1787, after a lot of discussion, Delaware became the first state to approve the Constitution. Pennsylvania, New Jersey, Georgia, Connecticut, and Massachusetts followed. After Maryland and South Carolina, only one more state was needed. On June 21, 1788, New Hampshire approved the Constitution: America would have a new government.

Who was the first president?

merica was ready for its new government. But it needed its first president. The famous general and leader of the Constitutional Convention, George Washington, was chosen unanimously. On April 30, 1789, George Washington took the oath to serve the young country and protect the even-younger Constitution. After Washington served as president for four years, he wanted to retire, but people convinced him to stay for another term. Washington agreed, but retired happily after four more years. Today, no president is allowed to serve more than two terms in office.

George Washington became the first President of the United States of America in 1789.

Has the Constitution changed?

The framers of the Constitution knew that people might need new laws in the future. If the Constitution were to last, people would need to be able to make changes. Changes to the Constitution are called amendments, and they can be added in two ways. The first way is for two-thirds of the states to call for another constitutional convention, where all of the states can suggest amendments. This has never happened.

The second way the Constitution can be amended is through Congress. If two-thirds of both the House of Representatives and the Senate vote for an amendment, then a vote goes to the state governments. If three-fourths of the states, 38, approve the amendment, it becomes law.

James Madison wrote the first ten amendments to the US Constitution. They are called the Bill of Rights.

What is the Bill of Rights?

The Constitution was in place, but some Americans thought people's rights weren't protected from the government strongly enough. So James Madison wrote amendments to be added to the Constitution. Ten passed and became known as the Bill of Rights.

- THE 1ST AMENDMENT guarantees that Americans have the rights to free speech, to practice their own religions or none at all, to write whatever they want, and to gather together and ask the government to change.

- THE 2ND AMENDMENT says that since Americans need a militia or national guard, people are allowed to own guns.

- THE 3RD AMENDMENT says that people don't have to give up their homes to soldiers.

- THE 4TH AMENDMENT says that the police cannot search people's homes without a warrant, or permission, from a judge, and that there has to be a good reason to get that warrant.

- THE 5TH AMENDMENT says that people who are accused of crimes have to be treated fairly.

- THE 6TH AMENDMENT says that trials for people accused of crimes have to be quick and fair and in front of a jury.

- THE 7TH AMENDMENT says that people get trials by juries in other, noncriminal trials.

- THE 8TH AMENDMENT protects people from being punished in cruel or unusual ways.

- THE 9TH AMENDMENT says that even if a right isn't listed in the Constitution, that doesn't mean that Americans don't have that right.

- THE 10TH AMENDMENT says that if a power isn't given to the federal government, then the state government should have it.

Can amendments be taken back?

Amendments were added after the Bill of Rights, and more can still be added today. Amendments can't be taken out of the Constitution, but they can be repealed, or reversed, by another amendment. You probably know that alcohol isn't still illegal. That's because the Twenty-first Amendment, which was added in 1933, repealed the Eighteenth Amendment. If individual states want to outlaw alcohol they can, but the federal government no longer bans it.

ve Demand JUSTICE

VOTES FOR WOMEN

VOTE FOR WOMEN

Women who marched for the right to vote were called "suffragettes." They won "suffrage," or, the right to vote, in 1920.

What are other famous amendments?

- THE 13TH AMENDMENT made slavery illegal and was added shortly after the end of the Civil War.

- THE 14TH AMENDMENT says that all citizens are equally protected under the law. The states have to treat them equally, too. State laws that treat different people differently have to be changed.

- THE 15TH AMENDMENT says that people can't be forbidden from voting based on the color of their skin or if they had ever been enslaved.

- THE 18TH AMENDMENT outlawed making and selling or transporting alcohol starting in 1920.

- THE 19TH AMENDMENT guaranteed women the right to vote in 1920.

- The most recent amendment says that if Congress votes to raise its members' pay, the new pay won't begin until after the next election. This amendment was added in 1992, but it was written by James Madison for the Bill of Rights in 1789. It took just under 203 years for the states to ratify it!

What is the future for the Constitution?

The United States Constitution has lasted into the 21st century. The hard work that the framers of the Constitution did during the long hot summer of 1787, and the power of debate, produced a durable, sturdy government. But the Constitution is also a living document that has changed as the United States has grown. Every new law is compared to the rules set up by the Constitution. So, in a way, framers like Madison, Franklin, and Washington are still helping to shape the country.

Just as the Constitution lays out the government's duty to the people, the people have a duty to the Constitution that they fulfill by voting. Every generation has to take responsibility for the government, which is why special attention is given to get young people involved. The 26th Amendment set the voting age at eighteen. It might seem far off now, but someday soon you will be able to vote. Just like the millions of people who have voted before you, it will be your chance to shape your country.

CONSTITUTION TIMELINE

1215, June	England's King John signs the Magna Carta, which outlines the rights of citizens. It would go on to influence the writers of the Constitution.
1775	The Revolutionary War begins. The American colonies fight to escape British rule.
1776	The Continental Congress meets and drafts the Articles of Confederation, which help the colonies manage themselves during the war.
1786	Tired of being in debt, the Massachusetts farmer Daniel Shays leads a rebellion against Massachusetts. Shays' Rebellion highlights the weakness of the Articles of Confederation.
1787, May	James Madison is the first to arrive in Philadelphia for the Constitutional Convention.
1787, September	George Washington is the first to sign the newly drafted Constitution on September 17, ending the Constitutional Convention.
1788	New Hampshire becomes the ninth state to ratify the Constitution, putting it into effect for the whole country.
1790, May	Rhode Island is the last of the thirteen original colonies to ratify the Constitution.
1791	The first ten amendments to the Constitution, called the Bill of Rights, are added all at once.
1865	The passage of the Thirteenth Amendment abolishes slavery except as punishment for a crime.
1868	The passage of the Fourteenth Amendment means that anyone born in the United States is a citizen.
1992	Originally written by James Madison to be included in the Bill of Rights, in 1789, the Twenty-seventh Amendment is finally ratified almost 203 years later.

For bibliography and further reading visit www.sterlingpublishing.com/good-question.